100 GREATEST SONGS of ROCK & ROLL

TENOR SAX

Music First

Available for

FLUTE, CLARINET, ALTO SAX, TENOR SAX, TRUMPET, HORN, TROMBONE, VIOLIN, VIOLA, CELLO

Note: The keys in this book do not match the other wind instruments.

The following songs have been omitted from this publication because of licensing restrictions:
Johnny B. Goode
Jumpin' Jack Flash
Kashmir
Rock and Roll
Sympathy for the Devil
Whole Lotta Shakin' Goin' On

ISBN 978-1-4803-4134-0

HAL•LEONARD®
CORPORATION
7777 W. BLUEMOUND RD. P.O. BOX 13819 MILWAUKEE, WI 53213

Visit Hal Leonard Online at
www.halleonard.com

ALL ALONG THE WATCHTOWER

TENOR SAX

Words and Music by
BOB DYLAN

Moderate Rock

ALL SHOOK UP

TENOR SAX

Words and Music by OTIS BLACKWELL
and ELVIS PRESLEY

AMERICAN PIE

TENOR SAX

Words and Music by
DON McLEAN

BEAT IT

TENOR SAX

Words and Music by
MICHAEL JACKSON

BLOWIN' IN THE WIND

TENOR SAX

Words and Music by
BOB DYLAN

BLUE SUEDE SHOES

TENOR SAX

Words and Music by
CARL LEE PERKINS

BORN TO BE WILD

TENOR SAX

Words and Music by
MARS BONFIRE

BOHEMIAN RHAPSODY

TENOR SAX

Words and Music by
FREDDIE MERCURY

BORN TO RUN

TENOR SAX

Words and Music by
BRUCE SPRINGSTEEN

BRIDGE OVER TROUBLED WATER

TENOR SAX

Words and Music by
PAUL SIMON

BROWN EYED GIRL

TENOR SAX

Words and Music by
VAN MORRISON

BROWN SUGAR

TENOR SAX

Words and Music by MICK JAGGER
and KEITH RICHARDS

CALIFORNIA DREAMIN'

TENOR SAX

Words and Music by JOHN PHILLIPS
and MICHELLE PHILLIPS

CALIFORNIA GIRLS

TENOR SAX

Words and Music by BRIAN WILSON
and MIKE LOVE

CRAZY

TENOR SAX

Words and Music by
WILLIE NELSON

A DAY IN THE LIFE

TENOR SAX

Words and Music by JOHN LENNON
and PAUL McCARTNEY

Moderately slow

DREAM ON

TENOR SAX

Words and Music by
STEVEN TYLER

EVERY BREATH YOU TAKE

TENOR SAX

Music and Lyrics by
STING

FIRE AND RAIN

TENOR SAX

Words and Music by
JAMES TAYLOR

FOR WHAT IT'S WORTH

TENOR SAX

Words and Music by
STEPHEN STILLS

FREE BIRD

TENOR SAX

Words and Music by ALLEN COLLINS
and RONNIE VAN ZANT

GIMME SOME LOVIN'

TENOR SAX

Words and Music by STEVE WINWOOD,
MUFF WINWOOD and SPENCER DAVIS

GLORIA

TENOR SAX

Words and Music by
VAN MORRISON

GOD ONLY KNOWS

TENOR SAX

Words and Music by BRIAN WILSON
and TONY ASHER

GOOD GOLLY MISS MOLLY

TENOR SAX

Words and Music by ROBERT BLACKWELL
and JOHN MARASCALCO

Moderately fast

GOOD VIBRATIONS

TENOR SAX

Words and Music by BRIAN WILSON
and MIKE LOVE

GREAT BALLS OF FIRE

TENOR SAX

Words and Music by JACK HAMMER
and OTIS BLACKWELL

A HARD DAY'S NIGHT

TENOR SAX

Words and Music by JOHN LENNON
and PAUL McCARTNEY

HEARTBREAK HOTEL

TENOR SAX

Words and Music by MAE BOREN AXTON,
TOMMY DURDEN and ELVIS PRESLEY

HEY JUDE

TENOR SAX

Words and Music by JOHN LENNON
and PAUL McCARTNEY

HOTEL CALIFORNIA

TENOR SAX

Words and Music by DON HENLEY,
GLENN FREY and DON FELDER

HOUND DOG

TENOR SAX

Words and Music by JERRY LEIBER
and MIKE STOLLER

(I Can't Get No)
SATISFACTION

TENOR SAX

Words and Music by MICK JAGGER
and KEITH RICHARDS

I GOT YOU
(I Feel Good)

TENOR SAX

Words and Music by
JAMES BROWN

I HEARD IT THROUGH THE GRAPEVINE

TENOR SAX

Words and Music by NORMAN J. WHITFIELD
and BARRETT STRONG

I WANT TO HOLD YOUR HAND

TENOR SAX

Words and Music by JOHN LENNON
and PAUL McCARTNEY

IMAGINE

TENOR SAX

Words and Music by
JOHN LENNON

IN THE MIDNIGHT HOUR

TENOR SAX

Words and Music by STEVE CROPPER
and WILSON PICKETT

JAILHOUSE ROCK

TENOR SAX

Words and Music by JERRY LEIBER
and MIKE STOLLER

Fast Rock

JUMP

TENOR SAX

Words and Music by EDWARD VAN HALEN,
ALEX VAN HALEN and DAVID LEE ROTH

LA BAMBA

TENOR SAX

By RITCHIE VALENS

LAYLA

TENOR SAX

Words and Music by ERIC CLAPTON
and JIM GORDON

LET IT BE

TENOR SAX

Words and Music by JOHN LENNON
and PAUL McCARTNEY

LET'S STAY TOGETHER

TENOR SAX

Words and Music by AL GREEN,
WILLIE MITCHELL and AL JACKSON, JR.

LIGHT MY FIRE

TENOR SAX

Words and Music by
THE DOORS

LIKE A ROLLING STONE

TENOR SAX

Words and Music by
BOB DYLAN

LONDON CALLING

TENOR SAX

Words and Music by JOE STRUMMER,
MICK JONES, PAUL SIMONON
and TOPPER HEADON

LOUIE, LOUIE

TENOR SAX

Words and Music by
RICHARD BERRY

Moderate Rock

2nd time, D.C. al Coda

CODA

MAGGIE MAY

TENOR SAX

Words and Music by ROD STEWART
and MARTIN QUITTENTON

MORE THAN A FEELING

TENOR SAX

Words and Music by
TOM SCHOLZ

MY GENERATION

TENOR SAX

Words and Music by
PETER TOWNSHEND

MY GIRL

TENOR SAX

Words and Music by WILLIAM "SMOKEY" ROBINSON
and RONALD WHITE

NO WOMAN NO CRY

TENOR SAX

Words and Music by
VINCENT FORD

PAPA WAS A ROLLING STONE

TENOR SAX

Words and Music by NORMAN WHITFIELD
and BARRETT STRONG

OH, PRETTY WOMAN

TENOR SAX

Words and Music by ROY ORBISON
and BILL DEES

PIANO MAN

TENOR SAX

Words and Music by
BILLY JOEL

PROUD MARY

TENOR SAX

Words and Music by
JOHN FOGERTY

PURPLE HAZE

TENOR SAX

Words and Music by
JIMI HENDRIX

RESPECT

TENOR SAX

Words and Music by
OTIS REDDING

Moderately

ROCK AROUND THE CLOCK

TENOR SAX

Words and Music by MAX C. FREEDMAN
and JIMMY DeKNIGHT

ROXANNE

TENOR SAX

Music and Lyrics by
STING

SEXUAL HEALING

TENOR SAX

Words and Music by MARVIN GAYE,
ODELL BROWN and DAVID RITZ

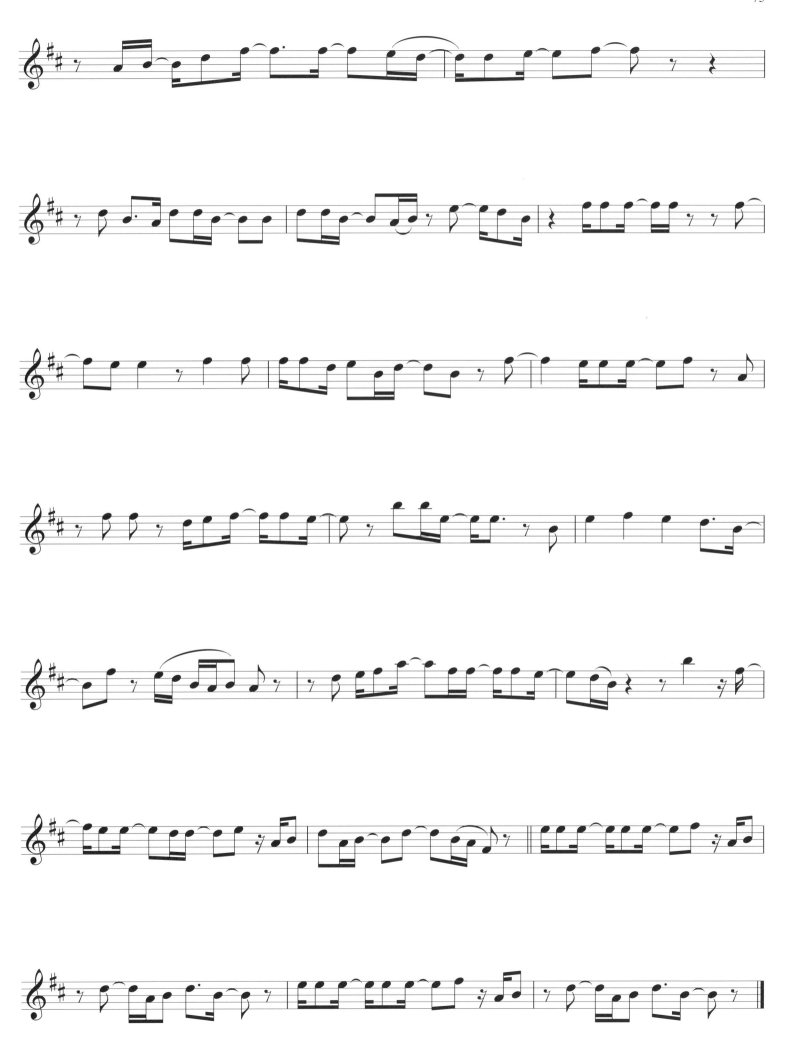

SHE LOVES YOU

TENOR SAX

Words and Music by JOHN LENNON
and PAUL McCARTNEY

(SITTIN' ON) THE DOCK OF THE BAY

TENOR SAX

Words and Music by STEVE CROPPER
and OTIS REDDING

SMELLS LIKE TEEN SPIRIT

TENOR SAX

Words and Music by KURT COBAIN,
KRIST NOVOSELIC and DAVE GROHL

SOMEBODY TO LOVE

TENOR SAX

Words and Music by
DARBY SLICK

SPACE ODDITY

TENOR SAX

Words and Music by
DAVID BOWIE

STAIRWAY TO HEAVEN

TENOR SAX

Words and Music by JIMMY PAGE
and ROBERT PLANT

STAND BY ME

TENOR SAX

Words and Music by JERRY LEIBER,
MIKE STOLLER and BEN E. KING

START ME UP

TENOR SAX

Words and Music by MICK JAGGER
and KEITH RICHARDS

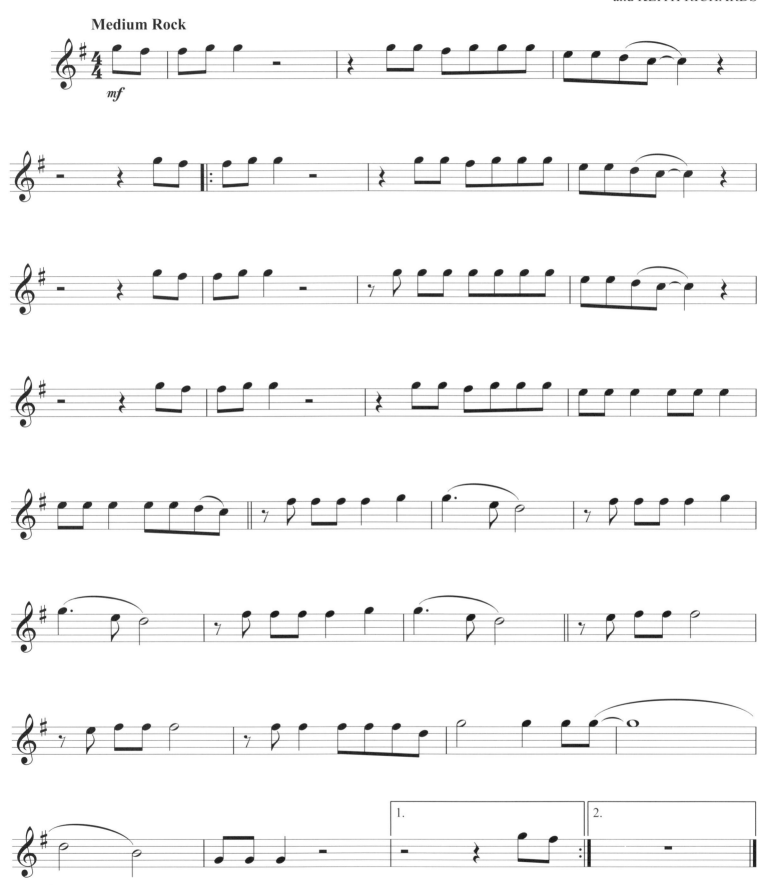

STRAWBERRY FIELDS FOREVER

TENOR SAX

Words and Music by JOHN LENNON
and PAUL McCARTNEY

Moderately slow

To Coda

D.C. al Coda
(no repeat)

CODA

1.

2.

Copyright © 1967 Sony/ATV Music Publishing LLC
Copyright Renewed
All Rights Administered by Sony/ATV Music Publishing LLC, 424 Church Street, Suite 1200, Nashville, TN 37219
International Copyright Secured   All Rights Reserved

STAYIN' ALIVE

TENOR SAX

Words and Music by BARRY GIBB,
ROBIN GIBB and MAURICE GIBB

SUITE: JUDY BLUE EYES

TENOR SAX

Words and Music by
STEPHEN STILLS

SUMMERTIME BLUES

TENOR SAX

Words and Music by EDDIE COCHRAN
and JERRY CAPEHART

SUNSHINE OF YOUR LOVE

TENOR SAX

Words and Music by ERIC CLAPTON,
JACK BRUCE and PETE BROWN

SUPERSTITION

TENOR SAX

Words and Music by
STEVIE WONDER

TANGLED UP IN BLUE

TENOR SAX

Words and Music by
BOB DYLAN

Moderately, in 2

THAT'LL BE THE DAY

TENOR SAX

Words and Music by JERRY ALLISON,
NORMAN PETTY and BUDDY HOLLY

THUNDER ROAD

TENOR SAX

Words and Music by
BRUCE SPRINGSTEEN

THE TWIST

TENOR SAX

Words and Music by
HANK BALLARD

TWIST AND SHOUT

TENOR SAX

Words and Music by BERT RUSSELL
and PHIL MEDLEY

WALK THIS WAY

TENOR SAX

Words and Music by STEVEN TYLER
and JOE PERRY

WE ARE THE CHAMPIONS

TENOR SAX

Words and Music by
FREDDIE MERCURY

WE'VE ONLY JUST BEGUN

TENOR SAX

Words and Music by ROGER NICHOLS
and PAUL WILLIAMS

WHAT'D I SAY

TENOR SAX

Words and Music by
RAY CHARLES

WHAT'S GOING ON

TENOR SAX

Words and Music by RENALDO BENSON,
ALFRED CLEVELAND and MARVIN GAYE

WHEN DOVES CRY

TENOR SAX

Words and Music by
PRINCE

WHOLE LOTTA LOVE

TENOR SAX

Words and Music by JIMMY PAGE,
ROBERT PLANT, JOHN PAUL JONES,
JOHN BONHAM and WILLIE DIXON

WILD THING

TENOR SAX

Words and Music by
CHIP TAYLOR

WON'T GET FOOLED AGAIN

TENOR SAX

Words and Music by
PETER TOWNSHEND

YESTERDAY

TENOR SAX

Words and Music by JOHN LENNON
and PAUL McCARTNEY

Moderately

YOU REALLY GOT ME

TENOR SAX

Words and Music by
RAY DAVIES

YOU SHOOK ME ALL NIGHT LONG

TENOR SAX

Words and Music by ANGUS YOUNG,
MALCOLM YOUNG and BRIAN JOHNSON

YOUR SONG

TENOR SAX

Words and Music by
ELTON JOHN and BERNIE TAUPIN